FAQ

TEEN LIFE™

FREQUENTLY ASKED QUESTIONS ABOUT

Peer Pressure

Rich
Juzwiak

ROSEN
PUBLISHING®

New York

Published in 2009 by The Rosen Publishing Group, Inc.
29 East 21st Street, New York, NY 10010
www.rosenpublishing.com

Library of Congress Cataloging-in-Publication Data

Juzwiak, Richard.
Frequently asked questions about peer pressure / Rich
Juzwiak.—1st ed.
    p.cm.—(FAQ: Teen Life)
Includes bibliographical references and index.
ISBN-13: 978-1-4042-1805-5 (library binding)
1. Peer pressure in adolescence—Juvenile literature. I. Title.
HQ799.2.P44J89 2009
305.235—dc22

                                                      2008000355

Manufactured in the United States of America

contents

CHAPTER one

WHAT IS PEER PRESSURE?

Usually, it is fun to be with friends. Friends enjoy activities together and trust one another. But what should you do when some of your friends begin to do things that make you uncomfortable, such as drinking, smoking, or using drugs? What if a friend asks you to help him or her cheat on a test? Situations like these can make you feel nervous or confused. Your friends can be persuasive, and it can be difficult to stand up to them. It can also make you doubt yourself. It's hard to know what to do.

Everyone wants to be accepted by people they admire. Some people, especially teens, will do things to fit in with a group, including drinking, doing drugs, lying to parents, rejecting childhood friends, and having unsafe sex. This pressure to do things that you might not do on your own is called peer pressure.

Friends are probably one's closest peers. Whether in a positive or negative way, friends can have tremendous influence and impact on one another.

Peer pressure can take many forms. It can be as open as some-one saying, "Don't be such a goody-goody" or "Everybody's doing it." It can also be subtler, such as unvoiced expectations by your friends about how to dress, act, or treat other people.

Nobody wants to admit that they are affected by peer pressure. They think that if they admit that peer pressure influences them, it will mean they're weak or they can't make up their own mind. The truth is that peer pressure can be difficult to resist, and we're all influenced by what others do and say.

Who Are Your Peers?

Anyone who is similar to you is considered your peer. Your peers may be other students in your school or other people your own age. If you play a sport, athletes who compete at your level are your peers. If you have a job as a stock person in a department store, people who work in stock are considered your peers. Unlike your parents or teachers, your peers are people who are in the same situation as you are. They often share similar experiences or lifestyles. Your friends are probably your closest peers. Friends may share common interests and enjoy doing certain things together.

Because you are likely to be influenced to some degree by the people with whom you surround yourself, it is important to choose your friends carefully. If you disagree with a decision that your friends are making—whether it is something you don't want to do or that goes against your personal or social values—it is important to make the decision that is right for you. You need to feel good about the choices you make. You and your friends don't always have to agree or have the same interests. In fact, a little diversity among friends can add to the enjoyment of the relationship.

Peer Pressure in Your Life

Peer pressure is what causes people to do things that are popular in order to fit in. This pressure can affect simple things, such as the way you dress, the music you listen to, or even whether or not you take drugs.

Keep in mind, too, that peer pressure is not always a bad thing. Sometimes, this pressure can have a positive impact on your life. For example, if you join a sports team, it is likely that you will be encouraged by your peers to be the best you can be. Joining the debate team may help you become a better student. Likewise, if you and your friends think that going to college is important, it may influence you to put more effort into studying. This is all positive peer pressure. On the other hand, if your group of friends thinks that stealing is cool and to fit in with them you also begin to steal, this is negative peer pressure. Your peers can have a positive influence when they motivate you to accomplish your goals. But they can also pressure you to do things that you do not want to do. This negative pressure may make you afraid to express an opinion that is different.

Choices

Growing up involves many changes. Attempting to figure out who you are and what you want to be may cause an enormous amount of stress. You are beginning to take control of your own life and make your own decisions. Sometimes, it is difficult to know what choices to make. People often look to their friends to help them make decisions.

A group of friends often shares a similar view of what is acceptable and what is not. Your peer group may seem to be following informal rules. There may be certain things that you have to do in order to fit in. You may feel that you should like certain music or dress in a certain way. Different groups have different preferences. Maybe your friends wear baggy clothes and have tattoos. Or perhaps they listen to country music. To you and your friends, these are just some of the distinctive qualities that make a person part of your group.

If the rules that your group follows fit in with the way you want to live your life, you will be content. However, if the rules of your group do not fit in with the choices you want to make—perhaps you want to do well in school and your friends have started cutting class a lot—it does not mean that you are not normal. It means only that you are a little different from those who are closest to you. Also, just because others do something does not mean that it is a good thing to do or that it is right. For example, if your friends use illegal drugs, it does not make those drugs any less illegal or any less harmful.

It may be difficult to convince yourself that your friends' behavior is not acceptable. If everyone is drinking, it can't be that big of a deal, right? Or, if all of the people you hang out with lie to their parents about where they go and what they're doing, then it must be OK if you lie to your parents and treat them poorly, right?

It is important, when you find yourself abiding by rules that you don't agree with, to step back and examine why you are going against your own convictions. It isn't easy to go against what everyone else does, but you should feel comfortable about the choices you make, and your friends should respect those choices. You do not need to be exactly like your friends. Learning to express your needs and values is a valuable skill that you will use throughout your life.

Friends usually share similar views or follow the same "rules." For instance, they might dress the same way, study or play a sport together, or listen to the same music.

Values

You are probably used to parents and teachers telling you what are right and wrong things to do. As you grow older, you try to discover values and opinions that are meaningful for you. Making decisions can be difficult. Often it is helpful to talk to friends who are experiencing similar problems. It may be easier to talk about your feelings when you can discuss them with friends. Your friends are people you can relate to and trust.

Because your friends' opinions are so valuable, they usually have a great influence over the decisions you make. Your friends can give you the emotional support you need to make it through tough times. They can make you feel comfortable and accepted. A sense of belonging and identifying can also increase your self-esteem, or what you think of yourself. Your friends trust you and talk to you about their problems. Maybe you have faced similar situations. You gain confidence as you try to help them figure out their problems.

Your peer group can greatly influence your values. For instance, if your friends feel that getting good grades is important, they may reinforce the idea for you. If the members of your group think that studying isn't necessary, you may let your grades slide to fit in with them. Or maybe you have never considered volunteering in the community before, but your new friends think that it is a good thing to do. In this way, your friends are influencing your values.

When you feel comfortable with the values that your friends have, positive peer pressure can be helpful. But it is important to recognize if the pressure from your friends becomes negative. You should pay close attention to situations in which your friends want to do things that do not agree with what you believe is right. When these situations arise, a person should decide which values are important to him or her, regardless of what friends think.

HOW DO I STAND STRONG AGAINST PEER PRESSURE?

Maintaining your individuality in the face of peer pressure can be difficult, especially as a teenager. Up until now, you have probably relied upon your family to help you decide what is right for you. They have guided your choices and passed along their values. Now is the time when you will be establishing independence from your parents. It's time for you to make your own choices. Your peers' opinions and values often become more important than those of your family members. This shift is what makes peer pressure so powerful.

It can be tough to stand firm regarding your beliefs when you are still trying to figure out what they are. Certainly, you want to be an individual, but you also want to fit in with your friends. And you must balance that with the expectations and rules of your family. Now is a critical time to assess yourself and learn to make choices

Pursuing your own interests, including sports, art, science, or writing, will help build your self-esteem and sense of individuality.

that enhance your life, not ones that stifle it or lead you down a path of self-destruction. You have a responsibility to yourself to decide what is best, now and for your future. Many of the choices you make today will affect the rest of your life.

To help you make good choices, explore the aspects of yourself that you like. Are you a talented painter? Take some art classes. Do you love to run in races? Find out when tryouts are for the track team. Do you like to write? Now would be a great time to discover the school newspaper. Pursuing your interests helps build your self-esteem and develop self-respect, which are important steps in resisting negative peer pressure. Take the example of a teen who wants to be a professional athlete. He has made a decision not to do drugs based on respect for himself as an athlete. He has established his own values. A supportive friend would respect his decision and want him to succeed.

Types of Negative Peer Pressure

The term "peer pressure" refers to any type of influence that your friends may have over you. Many times, teens are influenced by their peers to do things that result in negative consequences. This is negative peer pressure. Specifically, negative peer pressure refers to activities such as using drugs, alcohol, or cigarettes; vandalizing property; using violence against others; having sex before you are ready or having unsafe sex; stealing; or driving drunk.

Certainly, the opinions of your friends are important and you want to fit in with them. But if they are influencing you to do things that are destructive, illegal, or unhealthy, it might be time to reevaluate why you have chosen to surround yourself with these people. These types of activities can have a negative impact on the rest of your life, and you should take them very seriously. You could end up physically injured, in jail, responsible for the injuries of someone else, addicted to drugs, or worse.

Remember, the choice is always yours. Even if your friends make bad decisions, it does not mean that you have to go along with them. Unfortunately, however, your friends might not be

Negative peer pressure, especially when it involves drugs or alcohol, can lead to complications or trouble with the law. Above, a teenager is arrested after failing a breathalyzer test.

understanding when you assert an opinion that is different from theirs. They might begin to put more pressure on you or get angry with you. They might feel like you are judging them and resent you for that. Again, it might seem easier to simply go along with the crowd. It takes a lot of courage to stand up for yourself if what you think and do are different from what your friends think and do. If your friends will not accept you if you don't participate in activities that you know you shouldn't, it's probably time to reevaluate those friendships. True friends want the best for you and respect your decisions.

Too Much of a Good Thing

Most people assume that pressure to do well or strive for meaningful goals is always good. For example, if you want to do well in school, you will feel pressure to get good grades. But even positive peer pressure can go too far. If, for instance, you feel worthless unless you always earn As, you may suffer from putting too much pressure on yourself. Or, what if you want to become the best runner on the cross-country team so badly that you work out with an injury and end up being sidelined the entire season? This sort of pressure, although it is to pursue a positive goal, can turn negative if expectations are unrealistic or if they cause you to do things that are unreasonable, such as injuring yourself. It's important to keep your expectations in perspective. Make sure that you are striving for realistic goals and be sure to recognize your successes with as much intensity as you recognize your failures.

Influences on Your Decisions

Someone is more likely to be affected by peer pressure if he or she doesn't have respect for his or her own beliefs and interests. Building a solid sense of self helps you create healthy friendships. Otherwise, you end up relying upon others to make you feel good about yourself.

Someone with a strong sense of self chooses groups of friends that help him or her grow and complement his or her interests. There is not usually a search for direction or emotional support in this case. Leadership skills and goal-seeking are products of someone with a good sense of self. Self-confidence can help a person choose friends who will respect one's goals.

Self-Esteem and Family

Your family situation often has a great influence on your self-esteem. In healthy families, parents provide love, security, and encouragement. They help their children to grow up with confidence and self-worth. When you have confidence in yourself, you trust your instincts. You are more willing to try new things and are less afraid of making mistakes. You are also less likely to depend on a peer group to make decisions for you.

When families are not supportive, children get a different message. If little attention is paid to you at home, you may think that you don't matter or that you have failed in some way. You may be more likely to look at your peers for support. If you join a particular group because you doubt your own worth, you may

A supportive family can provide a great deal of love and encourage-ment, which adds to one's feelings of confidence and self-worth. Above, a father and son spend time talking with each other.

become more dependent on the group. That means you will be more likely to follow that group, regardless of what you think is right for you. It may be more difficult for you to resist peer pressure.

Fitting In, Standing Out

Within any group, each person generally has his or her position or status. Often, one person will stand out as the leader. He or she has the greatest influence on the rest of the group. Your status within your peer group will affect how much influence your peers have on you, as well as how much influence you have on them. If your only priority is to be like the leader because you admire that person, you are going to be greatly affected by the choices that person makes. If conformity is your ultimate goal in friendships, then you will probably be likely to do what other people in the group do. If, however, you strive toward being yourself, making choices based on your own sense of values, you will have greater self-confidence and will not be as affected by other people's decisions.

Myths and Facts

 All peer pressure is negative. Fact ➡ There are many types of peer pressure, and some are positive. Depending on your group of friends, peer pressure can cause you to do well on a sports team or strive for good grades.

 Peer groups must be made of similar, like-minded people. Fact ➡ While it's only natural to gravitate to people who are like you and who share similar interests, variety and differences can help you realize what is important to you and can help you expand your way of thinking.

 If the "rules" of your group do not match your own morals, you are abnormal. Fact ➡ It is OK to disagree with people in your peer group. In fact, if your peer group engages in damaging or illegal activity, it is in your best interest not to join in or agree. You are your own person—you don't have to do anything you don't want to do.

All positive peer pressure is helpful. Fact ●➤ Positive peer pressure can be stressful if it makes you worry all of the time. Even if it's pressing you to do something positive, peer pressure can have negative effects. For example, while getting good grades is a positive goal, too much pressure to meet unrealistically high expectations may actually be bad for your mental health.

Dating and having sex make you mature. If your friends are having sex, the time is right for you, too. Fact ●➤ If you aren't responsible with your relationship and sexual decisions, you aren't acting maturely. A person becomes mature not necessarily by what he or she does, but by the way he or she approaches situations and makes decisions. In addition, the decision to have sex is a personal one, not one that someone else can or should decide for you.

three

WHAT ARE SOME COMMON TEEN PRESSURES?

Your friends may or may not be pressuring you to do certain things. Often, a teenager's peers are the first group to introduce him or her to drugs, alcohol, and cigarettes. In addition, there are other pressures that many teens commonly face.

Drugs and Alcohol

Being pressured into doing something you don't want to do may end up resulting in problems. This is certainly true where drugs and alcohol are concerned. Drugs can cause you to do things you wouldn't normally do, things that you may later regret. Drugs are often addictive, bad for your health, and illegal. If you feel pressured into taking drugs, think about the person who is pressuring you. Is he or she really your friend? Or, does he or she just want someone to drink or do drugs with? The old saying "Misery loves company"

There can be a lot of peer pressure when it comes to drugs and alcohol. Remember that you don't need to drink or use drugs just because your friends are doing so. Only you should make that decision.

can be true where drugs are concerned. If a drug user can get other people to use with him or her, it may help that person feel better about himself or herself. Or, maybe the person wants to sell drugs to you. If the person can get you to use regularly, he or she will profit.

People who pressure you to use drugs are not doing so out of concern for you. They are motivated instead by self-interest, insecurity, or financial gain. A question to consider: Would this person want to hang out with you if you were not using drugs?

Or, would you want to hang out with him or her? If not, realize that this person is not your friend. If so, think about waiting until the person is sober and find ways to have fun together without drugs.

If you think that a friend has a drug problem, you should encourage him or her to seek help. Joining him or her by using drugs will only cause problems for both of you. You will be a better friend by helping your friend to stop using them.

Cigarettes

Maybe all of your friends smoke. If a friend starts smoking and tells you it's OK to do it, too, you are more likely to try smoking. In some peer groups, smoking is an unwritten rule. Friends may tell you that you are not cool if you don't smoke, or that you are a coward. Or, they might not say anything—they may just smoke all the time when you are with them. Either way, they may be influencing you to start smoking, too. Just remember that if they truly are your friends, they would accept your decision not to smoke, just as much as you respect their choice to smoke.

Cliques

Teens are often a part of a clique or group, which helps give them people to lean on and a sense of belonging. If you don't belong to the most popular group, you may feel excluded. You may not want their material things or even like these cliques or groups, but the attention, admiration, and influence they have can make you feel pressured to belong. You may find yourself pretending to care about things that you don't really have any interest in, such as sports or shopping, and you may find yourself conforming to the behavior of the group, just to belong.

Often cliques at school are a part of a social hierarchy, with the popular people having the most influence and the people who are not a part of this group having less. This can result in anguish and the people not in the popular group feeling badly about themselves. It can also result in people picking on those whom they perceive to have less influence.

Bullies and Their Victims

If you happen to be a part of the popular clique, be mindful of your behavior and your values. Just because your friends are cruel to others doesn't mean that you have to be. Try to empathize with the people whom your friends tease. Think about how badly you would feel, for example, if you had poor eyesight and needed glasses, and people at school made fun of you. Don't buckle down to any pressure that your friends may put on you to join in on their teasing. If people in your group feel that you should partake in the bullying, you might ask yourself if they really want to be around you and want your friendship. If they exert this sort of pressure on you to do something you don't want to do, then it seems likely that they may just want you to be a part of their group, to add to its size and level of intimidation, not necessarily because they like you as an individual. Remember that you are your own person, and you should do the right thing, not something that makes you feel bad.

Different cliques, or groups of people, often exist at school. These cliques might include the jocks, the popular kids, the geeks, and the artists, just to name a few.

If you feel that you or someone else is in physical danger or is experiencing extreme distress when you are at school, then you need to tell an adult you trust about what's happening. Talk to a teacher, school counselor, or some other grown-up who can give you assurance and sound advice.

Pressure Regarding Appearance

You may feel pressure to look the same as your peers. That might mean that you want to wear the kinds of clothes your peers are wearing, have the same haircut, or have the athletic body that some people have. If your parents are unable to afford to buy you the clothes that your peers are wearing, you might feel left out or embarrassed about the way you look. Or, you may exercise all the time to try to lose weight. Just like other types of peer pressures, the more confident you feel about your individuality, the less bad you'll feel about not being like others. One way to increase your self-esteem is to find ways in which you can emphasize your talents. If you are a good actor, try out for the school play. If you are articulate, run for a seat on student government. If you are a good writer, consider joining the school newspaper. If you feel good about yourself, then you won't fixate as much on what you perceive to be your pitfalls.

Dating and Sex

Many teenagers think that dating and having sex will make them seem mature. But dating and sex require responsibility

Friends often dress the same way or have similar hairstyles. Teens may feel stress or pressure to get the new clothes or shoes that everyone else is wearing.

first. Romantic and sexual feelings are a natural part of growing up. When you are ready to begin a sexual relationship, there are serious things that you need to think about. These include personal values, commitment, birth control, pregnancy, and sexually transmitted diseases (STDs).

Sex and Peer Pressure

Sex is an area in which peer pressure often comes into play. For example, someone might try to convince you to have sex with him or her, or tell you it's OK not to use a condom. Sometimes, a partner who wants to start a sexual relationship can be very insistent and try to convince you to do something that you don't really want to do. He or she may try to make you feel guilty for not having sex. You might be worried that he or she will break up with you if you don't have sex. If this happens, remember that everyone has the right to control his or her own body. A partner who cares about you will understand your decision. If someone does get angry with you or even breaks up with you because you won't have sex, it is a poor reflection on his or her character. You might feel embarrassed or hurt in such a situation, but in

There are many ways to enjoy an intimate relationship. Only you and your partner, not other peers, should determine when and if the time is right to become sexually active.

the long run that's much easier to deal with than a serious problem like an STD.

Peer pressure can also be less direct. If some of your friends are having sex, for instance, you might feel like you should be, too. Your friends may tell you about their experiences or offer you advice. If you are the only one of your friends who is not dating, you may feel left out. Or, maybe you feel that you are the only one of your friends who has not had sex.

Be Honest with Yourself

As a teen, your body undergoes a maturing process with many physical and emotional changes. You are beginning to see yourself as a person who is able to enjoy sexual behavior. Sexual behavior, however, includes much more than sexual intercourse. It can mean holding hands, kissing, cuddling, or touching. As you begin to explore your own sexuality, your peer group may have a strong influence on you. You will have to make important decisions about dating and sex. Before you listen to your friends' advice, however, look closely at what sexuality means to your peer group. Does your peer group use sex to:

- Be popular?
- Get even with someone else?
- Escape from problems?
- Improve self-esteem?
- Appear more grown-up?

Think about your own expectations regarding dating and sex. Ask yourself what you want and what you don't want. You may not agree with what your peer group is suggesting, and that's OK. Sex is a serious and personal matter.

If you do decide to become sexually active, you need to know about birth control and how to protect yourself from STDs. Whatever type of birth control you choose, it should offer dual-protection. First, it should protect against pregnancy. Just as importantly, it should protect against potentially deadly STDs like HIV (human immunodeficiency virus), the virus that causes AIDS (acquired immunodeficiency syndrome), as well as genital herpes and others. Effective contraception must serve these two critical purposes. Remember, however, that *no* birth control is 100 percent effective. Only abstaining from sex—not having sex—offers complete protection.

It can be difficult to abstain when your friends are not, but more and more teens are making the choice because of risks. You are the one who must live with the consequences of your choices, not your peer group. Make your decisions with that in mind.

Find the Right Time for You

Being different from the group can make anyone feel pressured to fit in. But you must be the one to make the actual decision. It is OK to postpone dating or sex. Whatever you choose, it is important for that decision to be your own.

Several measures can help you resist peer pressure. First and foremost, make decisions about sex before finding yourself in a relationship or sexual situation—and remind yourself why you made those decisions. They may be based on your beliefs and values, concerns for your health and future, or all of these. Keeping such thoughts in mind can help you stand firm in the face of peer pressure. Second, plan what to say before you're in "the moment." For example, you might tell your partner that respecting you means respecting your decision. You could also say that what you have is great, and you don't want to risk complicating it. Ultimately, if your partner or friend continues to do or say things that make you uncomfortable or doubt yourself, you may want to consider whether the relationship is worth holding onto.

Time alone can give you the chance to enjoy happy memories, think about what you would like to say to someone you care about, or deal with any troubles or worries that you may have.

Understand that you don't need a boyfriend or girlfriend to be happy and feel good about yourself. It is healthy to spend time alone. It can be a time to remember all those reasons why you are special on your own. Also, if you feel uncomfortable when you are alone, you may want to examine why. Perhaps there are some things that are bothering you that you have not wanted to face. Time alone can give you a chance to deal with the problems in your life.

There is nothing wrong with waiting for a time that feels more appropriate for you to enter a relationship or have sex. Not everyone is ready to have a serious relationship during the teenage years. But that doesn't mean you will never be ready. Decide what you feel is right for yourself. Relying too heavily on your peer group can make you ignore your own judgment. The decision to be sexually active is a choice that only you can make.

Date Rape

Being forced to have sex with someone against your will is rape. When this happens between people who know each other, it is called date rape. Rape is a violent crime. Being forced to have sex after you have said no is rape. Even if you are dressed in revealing clothing or have agreed to other kinds of touching, you still have the right to refuse sex. It doesn't matter if your date is drunk or high on drugs, it is still considered rape if you are forced to have sex after you've said no.

Sometimes, peer pressure may lead one person to rape another. This happens when the rapist feels as though his or her peer group expects him or her to have sex. The rapist becomes more interested in his or her reputation than the safety and emotional well-being of another person. When people act a certain way to fit in with a group's expectations, they can hurt themselves or others. Even though teens may feel pressured by their peers, they are still responsible for their own actions.

four

HOW DO I MAKE MY OWN DECISIONS AND ACCEPT RESPONSIBILITY?

Almost everyone can give an example of a phrase that implies peer pressure: "Everybody's doing it." "What are you, chicken?" "Aren't you cool?" All these statements are obviously pressuring. But you do not have to be directly challenged to do something in order to feel pressured. Even if nobody tells you to do things that the group does, you can feel pressured anyway. Teens feel pressured to fit in with their friends when they are afraid of being left out. Being different from the group can make some teens feel awkward.

It can be difficult to recognize and say no to unspoken peer pressure. If someone tells you to do something, you can always say no. But how do you say no when you haven't been asked? What do you do

Peer pressure does not always have to be spoken; it can also be implied. Take smoking, for example. If all of your friends smoke, it may start to seem cool or normal to do so, too.

when your group sets unspoken rules that you do not want to follow?

Peers don't always actively tell you to do things. They don't need to. If all of your friends smoke or do drugs, eventually you will begin to associate that habit with your group of friends. A habit you once thought was silly or stupid may start to seem cool. When each of your friends does something regularly, that action becomes legitimized in your mind. The actions of your friends will start to seem normal.

The Pressure to Belong

People often want to be like their friends. That's why the members of a peer group often dress similarly. They want to be identified with their friends. Often, people feel that being in a group gives them a certain identity. People who enjoy the same things, such as sports or art, will want to be in a group whose members have a reputation for being jocks or artists. Categories like these are stereotypes. Everybody has certain ideas about what a nerd, preppie, stoner, or hippie is like.

Trying to fit into a stereotype can be a type of unspoken peer pressure. In order to become a member of a group, or clique, you may feel that you have to do certain things. You may attempt to become the stereotype. This type of pressure can cause a lot of stress. Nobody is, or should strive to be, a stereotype. There are things that make everybody in a group different. Often, these stereotypes involve expectations that do not fit with who you really are. When this happens, you may feel pressured to do something that you do not truly want to do.

It can be hard to ignore unspoken peer pressure. But remember that your personality is unique and valuable. It can be fun to be with friends who have things in common with you. But you should not feel that everybody must be the same. Becoming a stereotype can hide some of the things that have made you who you are.

Discovering Yourself

As you mature, you may find yourself outgrowing past relationships. This is common, but it can be very difficult.

Changing your group of friends may mean parting with people you have been close to for many years. It might feel as if you are losing part of your identity.

People are constantly changing and growing. Interests and priorities will also change. If you find that you are losing interest in the things your friends want to do, or if you want to try something new, it may be time for a change. You can become friends with people whom you have more in common with. New friends may be what you need as you set new goals and think about the future.

Making Your Own Decisions

Sometimes, you may not want to do what your friends are doing. Maybe they're smoking, and you hate the smell of cigarette smoke. Maybe your group loves pop music, and you prefer jazz. Or, perhaps your friends make a habit of cutting classes, but grades are important to you. Some of your friends may do drugs, while you think using drugs is dangerous.

Everyone has felt pressured by his or her peers at some point. Even adults experience peer pressure. Peer pressure becomes negative when it causes someone to do something that is unhealthy or dangerous. People who allow themselves to be pressured by their peers are often afraid of being unpopular or alone. They may feel that keeping their friends, no matter what it takes, will make them feel better about themselves. But following the group in this way allows other people to make their decisions for them.

It is important to make your own decisions. If you hate the smell of cigarette smoke or are allergic to it, don't feel pressure to start smoking or be around people who smoke.

Saying No May Not Be Easy

It's easy for adults to tell you to "Just say no." But it's not always that simple. In fact, it can be hard to say no. You know that if you go along with whatever your friends are doing, your group is more likely to accept you. You also know that when you try to break away from the "rules," you risk being left out. Peer pressure makes these choices very difficult. But you do not have to go along with things that make you feel uncomfortable. You can't be expected to agree with everything that the rest of the group wants. Every person is unique.

If your peers are truly your friends, you should feel comfortable telling them that you don't want to do something like drinking, for example, or taking drugs. Just telling them no should be enough. If it isn't, be prepared to tell them why. Learn to say no without judging your peers; saying no is your choice, not theirs. You don't have to be aggressive, and you don't have to give them a lecture. Tell them that you're not interested, but be mindful not to insult them in the process. Whether you drink or do drugs isn't their decision, and it isn't your parents' decision. It's your decision, and yours alone.

Some Questions to Ask Yourself

There will always be people who will not take no for an answer. When you feel pressure to do anything you don't want to do, step back and ask yourself a few questions:

➤ Do I want to do this?
➤ Is this person worth throwing away my values for?

➤ Is this person going to like me less if I say no?

➤ How much do I care if this person likes me or not?

➤ Will this person respect me if I give in to his or her suggestions?

➤ Would I like someone less if he or she said no to me?

Different Ways of Saying No

You may find that the more you say no, the easier it becomes. As the saying goes, practice makes perfect. Visualize yourself saying no, and practice saying it at home. This will make it easier when the situation arises. Let's say you're at a party and someone offers you a drink or some drugs. Just say, "No, thanks," and chances are, whoever is offering it to you will leave it at that. Stay cool, and they will, too. If not, don't panic. There are ways to handle saying no. You can tell a joke, or change the subject. Say, "Let's go to the movies," or "Let's go to the mall and play video games." You can also say, "Forget it."

Be Confident in Your Decision

When you say no, say it like you mean it without sounding as though it's a big deal. A simple "No, thanks" will usually do, tossed off casually as if you were declining a cup of coffee. But if you are pressured further, stand firm. You'll be respected for it. If you sound wimpy or hesitant, you'll be treated accordingly.

Have a Reason Ready

It helps to be prepared with a reason to back up your decision. No matter what the circumstances, a simple explanation such as

There are lots of ways of saying no. Many times, a confident "No thank you" will do, or a simple reason like "I don't like the smell of cigarette smoke" is fine.

"I don't believe in cheating," "I don't like the taste of alcohol," or "I don't like being high" will show that you've thought about the situation and come to your own decision. Some teens use more detailed, personal reasons: "My mother is an alcoholic." People have a hard time arguing with a good excuse.

Don't Be Judgmental

Be fair in your refusal. Don't judge people harshly for their actions. In return, they likely won't judge you for declining to participate.

Make a Change

If you're feeling pressured, don't be afraid to leave the room, the party, or the situation. It's perfectly OK to do your own thing. If you fear for your safety, call a parent or another adult you trust. In addition, don't be afraid to change your friends if it comes to that. Do whatever you have to do to stay in control of your life.

Keeping Peer Pressure in Perspective

Although saying no won't always be easy, your challenge is to keep a proper perspective on your desire to fit in. You can lose sight of what you think is right when your peers are trying to get you to do something. You might be able to convince yourself that doing something that you know is wrong isn't a big deal. But if you get a bad feeling about something, it's for a reason. Trust your instincts and believe in yourself. Just because your friends tell you that something is all right doesn't make it OK.

It can be easy to lose perspective in the face of peer pressure. When you are being asked to do something you don't want to do, try to remember what you think is right and trust your own instincts.

Dare to Be Different

It takes a lot of courage to be yourself, but it can also bring you great satisfaction. Following your own beliefs will make you more independent. It will give you control over your actions.

Allowing yourself to be different helps you to figure out who you are. You might try new things that you never would have done if you only followed the group. Being independent allows you to find the activities, opinions, and tastes that you like the most and that best reflect your personality. It gives you the confidence to control your decisions and goals.

Ten Great Questions to Ask a Counselor

1 I don't agree with many of the ways my friends spend their time, but I do like them. Is it still worthwhile to maintain my friendships with them?

2 Who can I talk to if I disagree with the choices my friends are making?

3 What can I do to help build self-esteem so that I feel more confident about the choices I make?

4 All of my friends smoke, but I don't. How can I still hang out with them and keep from smoking?

5 How do I draw the line between setting high goals and setting expectations that are too high for myself?

6 My group of friends often picks on and bullies other kids at school. I don't join in, but I also don't stop them. Is my behavior wrong? What should I do?

7 My friend has started drinking every week-end. Should I interfere or just let him make his own decisions?

8 What are some ways to get away from peer pressure?

9 Can you suggest some local organizations or sources where I can meet people who share my interests?

10 Some of my friends are having sex. How do I know if I'm ready to be in a sexual relationship?

five

WHAT ARE SOME WAYS TO INFLUENCE PEERS IN A POSITIVE WAY?

Peer pressure is a two-way street. Although peer pressure has its negative side, young people can also influence each other in positive ways. Teenagers set examples for their friends when they encourage others to do their best in school; to stay away from smoking, drinking, and drugs; and to participate in fun, healthy activities.

Peer Counseling

Sometimes, it can be hard for teenagers to express their fears, problems, or deepest thoughts. In many schools, groups of teens become peer counselors (also called peer partners, peer helpers, natural helpers, or peer facilitators).

Peers are able to relate to what other young people are going through because they have experienced similar things. Therefore, a friend or peer counselor can be a great source of comfort.

These young people are trained to listen and respond to their teenaged peers.

Peer counselors can relate to what other young people are going through. They learn to be sensitive to the emotional needs of others and help their schoolmates to talk about their feelings. They also help them with decisions and show them what options are available.

Peer counselors can talk about many kinds of problems. Teens speak with them about relationships with parents or friends. They talk about pressures to drink or have sex. Peer counselors may hear stories of depression, loneliness, or abuse. Peer counselors can offer commonsense advice. Troubled students may look to counselors for suggestions. For other young people, just being able to talk about their concerns improves the quality of their lives.

Resolving Conflicts

Students Against Violence Everywhere (SAVE) and Peace by PEACE are two popular programs that are used today in many schools to help combat school violence. Both programs use peer mediation to stop violence. Teens who participate as mediators are trained to listen to other students and to help them resolve conflicts. Instead of using fists or weapons to solve arguments, students sit down and talk to one another calmly. They try to work things out with the help of a mediator. Many high schools involved in these programs have seen their levels of violence drop dramatically, easing tension and pressure for everyone.

Other groups throughout the country have been successful in working with students. SADD (Students Against Destructive Decisions) uses positive peer pressure to inform young people about the dangers of substance abuse, violence, impaired driving, and depression and suicide.

Groups like these help teens to cope with life's pressures while learning problem-solving skills. Teens involved in these groups also learn to be supportive of others. Most of all, they gain maturity and independence. They feel a sense of responsibility to other young people who are looking to them for support and direction at difficult times in their lives.

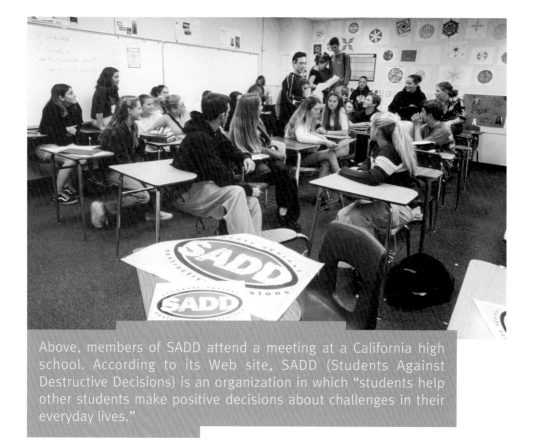

Above, members of SADD attend a meeting at a California high school. According to its Web site, SADD (Students Against Destructive Decisions) is an organization in which "students help other students make positive decisions about challenges in their everyday lives."

Feeling Good About Yourself

Work at thinking positively about yourself. Developing positive self-esteem can help you to resist pressure from friends. Positive self-esteem allows you to feel good about yourself, regardless of what others think. Look at all the things that you do well; maybe you can paint, sing, dance, play basketball, or make people laugh. Your talents can make you feel better about yourself and allow others to appreciate you for who you are.

Developing strong, positive self-esteem is one of the best ways to resist unwanted peer pressure and feel good about yourself.

Remember that other people are there for you if you need help. You can talk about your problems with your parents, friends, teachers, counselors, or religious leaders. Set goals for yourself. Don't make them unreachable—set goals you know you can achieve. For instance, a goal could be getting a grade higher than a C on your next history test. Congratulate yourself when you meet that goal.

Do things that make you feel good about yourself, such as trying out for a school play, volunteering to help behind the scenes if you're shy, or starting a hobby like playing the guitar. Helping others and developing your own skills will make you feel good about yourself. A part-time job can increase your sense of responsibility and independence.

It is better to have positive self-esteem than to depend on the approval of others. You will gain more confidence and control over your life. You will have the power to accept or reject what others think of you. Be proud of who you are and what you can accomplish.

You Can Do It

Being mature and acting responsibly are two of the most difficult things that can be asked of anyone. Learning to trust your own judgment can be a stressful, but rewarding, experience. Don't let others pressure you into doing things that are not right for you. Make your own decisions.

Being mature means having the ability to be both a good friend and an independent individual. It can be fun to be part of a group, but be aware if friendships are no longer comfortable. This may happen if your friends begin to do things that you do not agree with. Remember that you are always in control and have other choices. The most important element is to have a strong sense of your own individuality.

abstain To deliberately choose not to do something.

AIDS (acquired immunodeficiency syndrome) A disease of the immune system that is caused by the HIV virus.

articulate Able to express ideas and thoughts clearly.

assert To declare or state something as being true.

clique A group of people, usually a peer group, that shares common interests and is perceived as being exclusive.

conformity Going along with what others are doing in order to be liked or accepted by them.

date rape Sex between two people who know each other in which one person is forced.

diversity A variety of something like style or opinion.

emotional support Listening to and providing encouragement to someone with regard to his or her feelings.

empathize To understand and identify with another person's feelings or situation.

hierarchy Categorization of members of a group according to importance.

HIV (human immunodeficiency virus) A virus that destroys the immune system's helper T cells, the loss of which causes AIDS. HIV is transmitted in infected blood, commonly through intravenous drug use and in bodily secretions during sexual intercourse.

individuality A specific characteristic that distinguishes one person or thing from another.

instincts Strong motivations or impulses that are natural and intrinsic.

legitimized Argued or proven that an action is lawful or reasonable.

mediator Someone who works with the parties involved in a dispute and helps them try to reach an agreement.

peer group A group of friends or classmates who have things in common.

self-esteem Confidence in your self-worth or merit as an individual.

status One's position or rank in relation to others.

stereotype An oversimplified, standardized idea or image that one person or group has about another person or group.

stifle To prevent or limit the development of something.

values The beliefs that a person holds.

Al-Anon and Alateen

1600 Corporate Landing Parkway

Virginia Beach, VA 23454-5617

(888) 4AL-ANON (425-2666)

Web site: http://www.al-anon.org
  This organization assists alcoholics and their families via
  group support.

American Social Health Association

P.O. Box 13827

Research Triangle Park, NC 27709

(919) 361-8400

Web site: http://www.ashastd.org
  The Web site of this organization includes information on
  sexually transmitted diseases.

Boys & Girls Clubs of America

National Headquarters

1275 Peachtree Street NE

Atlanta, GA 30309-3506

(404) 487-5700

Web site: http://www.bgca.org
  The Boys and Girls Clubs of America offer young people a
  safe and supportive place to go for recreational activity
  and personal development.

National Association of Peer Programs (NAPP)

P.O. Box 10627

Gladstone, MO 64188-0627

(877) 314-7337

Web site: http://www.peerprograms.org

  NAPP helps establish, train, supervise, maintain, and evaluate peer programs.

National Association for Self-Esteem

P.O. Box 597

Fulton, MD 20759

Web site: http://www.self-esteem-nase.org

  This self-esteem organization offers a wealth of resources on its Web site. Rate your self-esteem, look for answers to frequently asked questions, and find links to other resources.

Operation Respect

2 Penn Plaza, 5th Floor

New York, NY 10121

(212) 904-5243

Web site: http://www.dontlaugh.org

  Operation Respect works to assure a respectful, safe, and compassionate climate of learning for youth that is free of bullying, ridicule, and violence.

Peace by PEACE

c/o Cindy Warner

321 West 54th Street, No. 510

New York, NY 10019

Web site: http://www.peacebypeace.org/pxp
This organization is dedicated to teaching peace to today's youth, including encouraging volunteerism.

Peer Resources
1052 Davie Street
Victoria, BC V8S 4E3
Canada
(800) 567-3700 or (250) 595-3503
Web site: http://www.peer.ca
Peer Resources provides educational resources and training to establish or strengthen peer mediation and mentor programs in schools and communities.

Students Against Destructive Decisions (SADD)
255 Main Street
Marlborough, MA 01752
(877) SADD-INC (723-3462)
Web site: http://www.sadd.org
SADD uses positive peer pressure to inform young people about the dangers of substance abuse, violence, impaired driving, and depression and suicide.

Students Against Violence Everywhere
    (National Association of SAVE)
322 Chapanoke Road, Suite 110
Raleigh, NC 27603
(866) 343-SAVE (7283)
Web site: http://www.nationalsave.org

This student-driven organization promotes peace through school and community activities.

YouthLaunch
7756 Northcross Drive, Suite 203
Austin, TX 78757
(800) 875-1862
Web site: http://www.youthlaunch.org
YouthLaunch provides service opportunities through which participants gain knowledge, learn skills, improve self-esteem, and develop a sense of social responsibility.

Web Sites

Due to the changing nature of Internet links, Rosen Publishing has developed an online list of Web sites related to the subject of this book. This site is updated regularly. Please use this link to access the list:

http://www.rosenlinks.com/faq/pepr

For Further Reading

Cherniss, Hilary, and Sara Jane Sluke. *The Complete Idiot's Guide to Surviving Peer Pressure for Teens.* Indianapolis, IN: Alpha Books, 2002.

Desseta, Al, M.A., ed., and Educators for Social Responsibility. *The Courage to Be Yourself: True Stories by Teens About Cliques, Conflicts, and Overcoming Peer Pressure.* Minneapolis, MN: Free Spirit Publishing, Inc., 2005.

Drew, Naomi. *The Kids' Guide to Working Out Conflicts: How to Keep Cool, Stay Safe, and Get Along.* Minneapolis, MN: Free Spirit Publishing, Inc., 2004.

Espeland, Pamela. *Life Lists for Teens: Tips, Steps, Hints, and How-Tos for Growing Up, Getting Along, Learning, and Having Fun.* Minneapolis, MN: Free Spirit Publishing Inc., 2003.

Hatchell, Deborah. *What Smart Teenagers Know . . . About Dating, Relationships, and Sex.* Santa Barbara, CA: Piper Books, 2003.

Koubek, Christine Wickert. *Friends, Cliques, and Peer Pressure: Be True to Yourself* (Teen Issues). Berkeley Heights, NJ: Enslow Publishers, 2002.

Lawton, Sandra Augustyn. *Drug Information for Teens: Health Tips About the Physical and Mental Effects of Substance Abuse.* Detroit, MI: Omnigraphics, 2006.

Macavinta, Courtney, and Andrea Vander Pluym. *Respect: A Girl's Guide to Getting Respect & Dealing When Your Line Is Crossed*. Minneapolis, MN: Free Spirit Publishing, Inc., 2005.

Painter, Carol. *Friends Helping Friends: A Handbook for Helpers*. 2nd ed. Minneapolis, MN: Educational Media Corporation, 2003.

Rue, Nancy R. *Everything You Need to Know About Peer Mediation* (Need to Know Library). New York, NY: Rosen Publishing Group, 2001.

Seaward, Brian Luke, Ph.D. *Hot Stones & Funny Bones: Teens Helping Teens Cope with Stress & Anger*. Deerfield Beach, FL: Health Communications, Inc., 2002.

Slavens, Elaine. *Peer Pressure: Deal with It Without Losing Your Cool*. Toronto, ON: Lorimer, 2004.

Webber, Diane. *Your Space: Dealing with Friends and Peers* (Scholastic Choices). New York, NY: Franklin Watts, 2008.

Index

About the Author

Rich Juzwiak is a writer who lives in Brooklyn, New York.

Photo Credits

Cover © www.istockphoto.com/Robert Churchill; p. 5 © www.istockphoto.com/Chris Schmidt; p. 9 © www.istockphoto.com/Li Kim Goh; pp. 13, 26 © Shutterstock.com; p. 15 © Joe Raedle/Getty Images; p. 18 © www.istockphoto.com/Aldo Murillo; p. 23 © Bill Aron/PhotoEdit; p. 28 © Peter Cade/Iconica/Getty Images; pp. 29, 44 © www.istockphoto.com/Izabela Habur; p. 32 © www.istockphoto.com/Mikhail Nekrasov; p. 36 © John Birdsall/The Image Works; p. 39 © www.istockphoto.com/Roberta Osborne; p. 42 © T. Bannor/Custom Medical Stock Photo; p. 48 © J.B.S.I./Custom Medical Stock Photo; p. 50 © Grantpix/Newscom.com; p. 51 © www.istockphoto.com/Eileen Hart.

Designer: Evelyn Horovicz; Photo Researcher: Amy Feinberg